The Highs *and* Lows *of* Life

POETIC BLESSINGS

Margie Shade Nelson

WESTBOW
PRESS®
A DIVISION OF THOMAS NELSON
& ZONDERVAN

WestBow Press books may be ordered through booksellers or by contacting:

WestBow Press
A Division of Thomas Nelson & Zondervan
1663 Liberty Drive
Bloomington, IN 47403
www.westbowpress.com
844-714-3454

Because of the dynamic nature of the Internet, any web addresses or links contained in this book may have changed since publication and may no longer be valid. The views expressed in this work are solely those of the author and do not necessarily reflect the views of the publisher, and the publisher hereby disclaims any responsibility for them.

Any people depicted in stock imagery provided by Getty Images are models, and such images are being used for illustrative purposes only. Certain stock imagery © Getty Images.

Scripture taken from the King James Version of the Bible.

Scripture quotations taken from The Holy Bible, New International Version® NIV® Copyright © 1973 1978 1984 2011 by Biblica, Inc. TM. Used by permission. All rights reserved worldwide.

Scripture taken from the New King James Version® Copyright © 1982 by Thomas Nelson. Used by permission. All rights reserved.

Scripture quotations are from the ESV® Bible (The Holy Bible, English Standard Version®), copyright © 2001 by Crossway, a publishing ministry of Good News Publishers. Used by permission. All rights reserved.

ISBN: 978-1-6642-0671-7 (sc)
ISBN: 978-1-6642-0670-0 (e)

Print information available on the last page.

WestBow Press rev. date: 10/05/2020

DEDICATION

This book is dedicated to all who have experienced or are now experiencing the highs and lows of life. Know that the same God who holds you when you are on the mountain, is the same God who holds you in the valley. May you be blessed.

CONTENTS

The Highs and Lows of Life

Yesterday the sky was blue
The sun was very bright
And somewhere in between the two
My restless heart took flight
It soared among the trees so high
Then in the valley landed
The force became so powerful
That I could hardly stand it
I cried, Dear God, what's happening?
Why did you let me go?
His reply returned to me
Because I love you so
I take you through the highs and lows
To show you what you're made of
That even though you're brave at times
There're still things you're afraid of
For if I never gave you night
And only gave you day
You would never seek my face
Neither would you pray
It's only in the darkness
That you seek the light
It's only in the valley
That you learn to fight
It's only when you're broken
That you need to mend
Now this is when you make me
Your Savior and your Friend.

In the world ye shall have tribulation: but be of good cheer;
I have overcome the world. John 16:33 KJV

GOD IN DRY PLACES

The desert is dry
I'm stuck in the sand
I'd like to get out
I know that I can
I've fasted and prayed
I've cried for hours
Longing for shade
And praying for showers
This journey I'm on is draining me dry
But I won't give up, I'm still going to try
A God in dry places I know You to be
You never give up on rescuing me
So for every person in a drought
Dealing with the pain
There is One to bring you out
And Jesus is His name.

"For His anger endures but a moment; in his favour is life: weeping may endure for a night, but joy cometh in the morning." Psalms 30:5 KJV

THEN CAME JESUS

My life was once a total mess
It seemed beyond repair
I had no one to turn to
No one seemed to care
I reached beyond my circumstance
When others thought why bother
Jesus came through for me
And now I call Him Father
My past had all but shattered me
Filled with shame and sin
Jesus came and rescued me
And now I call Him Friend
Things will come our way
That may or may not please us
But one thing is for certain
We can always count on Jesus.

INCLUDE GOD

The chances we take
The things we do
Decisions we make that don't include You
Will soon remind us
We've heard the wrong voice
Walked the wrong road
Made the wrong choice
Lord please help us to try this again
This time with You from beginning to end
Lord please help us to heed what You say
So we choose the right road
And go the right way.

MORE THAN A CONQUEROR

The enemy tries with all its force
To get you confused and throw you off course
But just stay focused keep your eyes on the Light
And know that the battle is not yours to fight
You may be in it but you're not alone
God wouldn't leave you to fight on your own
Keep walking with Jesus our Savior nonstop
And I guarantee you'll come out on top.

Yet in all things we are more than conquerors through Him who loved us. Romans 8:37 NKJV

A New Creature

No one but you Lord
No one but You
Can take something old
And make it new
You polish and buff it
With just the right force
Then straighten it up
And set it on course
You seal every crack
Together with gold
Then place it out front
Shiny and bold
A godly vessel
To carry Your word
Throughout the world
For it to be heard.

Therefore if any man be in Christ, he is a new creature: old things are passed away; behold, all things are become new. II Corinthians 5:17 KJV

Make the Lord Your Choice

It matters not how many times
You've gone against God's will
The only thing that matters
Is that He loves you still
He's waiting now with open arms
Bidding you to come
Longing to forgive you
For the wrongs you've done
Harden not your heart
The day you hear His voice
Choose to live forever
Make the Lord your choice
Tomorrow isn't promised
Today is now at hand
Choose to walk with Jesus
And not the path of man.

While it is said: "Today, if you will hear His voice, Do not harden
your heart as in the rebellion." Hebrews 3:15 NKJV

Your Day Will Come

Your day will come
But we don't know when
It won't matter where you are
It won't matter where you've been
It won't matter if you're brilliant
It won't matter if you're dumb
As surely as you live
Your day is going to come
It won't matter if you're rich
It won't matter if you're poor
You can bet your day is coming
If you live just one day more
When sickness hits your body
And healing has to wait
You'll sit out on the sidelines
And not participate
You'll watch the world around you
Enjoy the sunny day
And you will be reminded
Of when you used to play
You'll then return home
Sit in your easy chair
Or kneel beside your bed
And offer up a prayer
Like Lord please help me
I'm really very sick
Help me overcome this
Help me not to quit
Sometimes we learn lessons
Better off the track
By sitting on the sidelines
Or laying on our backs.

COME TO JESUS

I know I can't reach everyone
But God knows I've tried
Through many prayers
I've prayed for you
And many tears I've cried
I value what you mean to me
So hear my humble plea
Please give your life to Jesus Christ
And let Him set you free
Tomorrow isn't promised
Today is fading fast
Ask Jesus to forgive your sins
Future, present, past
Be willing to surrender
Your life into His Hands
And let Him resurrect you
And work in you His plans
Darkness has to flee
When Light enters a room
Jesus is the Light
Now let His presence bloom.

*While it is said: "Today, if you will hear His voice, Do not harden
your heart as in the rebellion." Hebrews 3:15 NKJV*

THE GOOD LIFE

Be strong
Live long
Love God
And love people.

"And now these three remain: faith, hope, and love. But the greatest of these is love".
I Corinthians 13:13 NIV

POETIC TOUCH

Poetry flows
When the Hands of God
Caresses the soul.

STEAL AWAY

When I make time to steal away it does my heart good
To bow before my Father's throne and know I'm understood
My faith becomes stronger my way becomes clear
Suddenly I'm unafraid He takes away my fear
Life is unpredictable but Jesus Christ is sure
So when I go through suffering I know He has the cure
Never will I walk alone a road I've never been
Without my loving Father, my Savior, and my Friend.

Be Strong in the Lord

Life is a challenge and you mustn't choose
To go it alone or else you will lose
The battle before you is already fought
The truth is God's Word that you have been taught
Walk in His likeness give Him the glory
Don't be afraid to share His story
A wavering faith will not stand the test
You must be bold and give it your best
Regardless of life's reflections of doubt
Don't let it put your candle out
You've started the race now finish it well
Stay focused on God and you will prevail.

Don't Give Up Now

This road is hard to travel
It's dark although it's day
I'm stumbling in it's gravel
Please Father lead the way
The sun seems nonexistent
But Your Word is true
Help me be persistent
In following after You
My energy is fading
Hope is almost gone
Once again I come to You
Please help me carry on
A shadow's overcome me
Help me to endure
You said You'ld never leave me
I know You're here for sure
Get me through this battle
Help me win this fight
Give to me the strength I need to make it through the night
If I hold out till tomorrow a change is going to come
And I'll be glad I waited to see the victory won.

"But they that wait upon the Lord shall renew their strength; they shall mount up with wings as eagles; they shall run, and not be weary; and they shall walk, and not faint." Isaiah 40:31 KJV

ONCE BROKEN

Woman, broken, little girl
Why are you hurting so?
Did someone come and steal your joy
A long time ago?
Did they break your heart in pieces?
Did they fail at being your friend?
Did they glue it back together
Then broke it yet again?
Are you living in a chamber
With issues unresolved?
Are you trying not to claim it
So that others aren't involved?
Can you own up to the truth?
Can you own up to the shame?
Can you give to God your weaknesses
And let Him have your pain?
Are you going through the motions
As you're holding back your tears?
Are you blocking out your vision
So that you won't face your fears?
Woman, broken, little girl
God's going to bring you through
Ask me how I know
For I once was broken too.

He heals the brokenhearted and binds up their wounds. Psalms 147:3 ESV

In Times Past

Screaming voices, many choices
Sores are oozing, Dad's abusing
Broken skin in hidden places
Tears roll down her siblings' faces
Moma speaks but Moma loses
She too gets some of the bruises
Noise increases, ears start ringing
To Moma's waist the youngster's clinging
The belt starts swinging then you're down
Being beaten on family ground
No one dared to say a word
To call the cops was rarely heard
They soothed each others' wounds of pain
Full of hate and so ashamed
Each one holding to their word
Pretending that they never heard
The cries from children being abused
For small mistakes they didn't choose
Home was like a prison then
Filled with pain provoked by sin
Freedom days seemed far away
And every night she'd kneel and pray
God please take me out of here
I do not want to live in fear
Suddenly her life was changed
She got aboard the freedom train
Glad to be out on her own
From the hurt that she had known
Now sometimes when looking back
She thinks of all the love she lacked
About the things she didn't do
That might have helped their family through
She dared not ruin the family name

Instead she hid her scars of pain
Those were some difficult years
Hiding the pain and withholding tears
Love seemed distant then
But today they're the closest
They've ever been
It's so amazing what God can do
When you give to Him your sorrows too.

He heals the brokenhearted and binds up their wounds. Psalms 147:3 ESV

Don't Be Defeated

The struggle is real
But stay in the fight
Don't ever give up
No matter the plight
The fact that you're living
Is proof you'll survive
You've faced countless storms
And came out alive
So keep pressing forward
To the new day ahead
Waiting to greet you
When you awake in your bed
Let nothing defeat you
Trust God instead
For He is in control.

REACH HIM LORD

You're slipping son
You're slipping
And I hate to see you slide
I hate seeing you suffer
On this vicious ride
But there is One who understands
The problems that you face
You're forever in His plans
And forever in His grace
I see you spiral upward
I see you spiral down
You're like a rollercoaster
That just keeps spinning round
Oh, if I could reach you
There in your addiction
I would love to free you
From this horrible affliction
Only God knows
that my praying won't cease
Until He delivers you
And gives you His peace
Life will get better
God answers prayers
So know that He hears you
And know that He cares.

He heals the brokenhearted and binds up their wounds. Psalms 147:3 ESV

God is in Control

Crazy thoughts may come and go, but God is in control
Nothing stops a child of God when Heaven is his goal
Do not succumb to OCD, nor let it have its way
Obsessions and compulsions may come but not to stay
God knows and understands the battles that we fight
He's forever with us, we're always in His sight
Do not let your OCD destroy and bring you down
Place your trust and faith in God; let His grace abound
Obstacles will come your way that you will have to face
Which are to be expected, along this Christian race
But what you must remember is that God is greater still
And will give to you the victory as you walk within His will.

Thou wilt keep him in perfect peace, whose mind is stayed on thee: because he trusteth in thee. Isaiah 26:3 KJV

Keep Holding On

I'm holding on in faith as You're holding on to me
The road which I will travel is one I cannot see
Because Your love is constant I'm forever in Your hands
Nothing happens to me unless it's in Your plans
Bless me and protect me with armor and with might
Lord please go before me and help me win this fight
The enemy's attacking trying to bring me down
Give me what I'm lacking help me stand my ground
Your grace and mercy is sure to get me through
Now help me not to focus on my problem but on You.

BE REAL

Come real before the Father
There's nothing He can't see
There's no place you can go
To hide yourself from Thee
His love is ever present
His mercy's proven true
His grace is sufficient
In helping you get through
When life attempts to break you
And knock you to the ground
Our Father won't forsake you
He'll never let you down
So let us not grow weary
When going through a trial
It's only temporary
It's only for a while.

Fit for the Fight

Fit for the Kingdom
Fit for the fight
I've come out of darkness into the light
Others before me keep wasting time
Looking for treasure but I have found mine
Jesus Christ has set me free
Way back then on Calvary
I am not ignorant of what He can do
What He's done for me He will do for you
Keep seeking Him day by day
He'll make His presence known
And when you let Him in your heart
You'll never walk alone.

I Feel You

I know what it's like to be broken to pieces
To be shattered like glass and treated like feces
I know what it's like from the places I've been
To come through a storm then face one again
I know what it's like to have foolish pride
To follow the crowd just for the ride
I know what It's like to ignore God's plan
Then suffer the blow from His mighty hand
I know a lot but not enough
God please take my broken stuff
Fix it up and make it new
Reminding me that's what You do
Fix it Lord and help me be
More like You and less like me.

TRUE FREEDOM

Salvation is free you can be too
When He died for me He died for you
There's nothing too difficult you can't reject
No sin too large to forgive and forget
Whatever you're facing, no matter the plight
Stay steadfast in Jesus, He'll make it alright
It's valid to say that you're given a choice
To accept Christ as Lord or to ignore His voice.

LET GOD HELP

There are people hurting
Who don't know what to do
And when they come to me for help
I point them to You
There is no one stronger to lift the load we bear
Nor anyone greater to whom we can compare
You're Alpha and Omega
Beginning and the End
Anywhere we go You've already been
You're the Lilly of the Valley
The Bright and Morning Star
Lord of Lords
King of Kings
Yes, that's who You are
For all the hurting people
Who feel all hope is gone
He's with you in the valley
And will help you carry on.

TRUTH

You can't have a testimony without an experience
You can't have an experience without life
And you can't have life without Christ.

MORE OF YOU LORD

Thank you Lord for letting me see
It's all about You and not about me
In the beginning You made it clear
That You control the atmosphere
Your wisdom and knowledge are beyond reach
No matter how we pray and preach
For what we have great or small
Belongs to You
You own it all
The poetry I like to write
Comes from You, You give insight
So keep me true and well aware
That when I kneel in fervent prayer
My greatest praise extends to You
Nothing less will ever do
I love You Lord
Now help me be
More like You
And less like me.

FULLY ALIVE

Where You lead I'll follow
Where You take me I'll go
Whether high upon the mountain
Or in the valley low
There's nothing I can't conquer
With You by my side
Every day that I live
I am fully alive.

OPEN ARMS

God's waiting for people to give Him their lives
Sisters, brothers, husbands, and wives
He's earnestly trying to reach out and touch
His lovely creation He loves so much
He wants us to follow, trust and obey
To expect an answer when we pray
He wants us to know Him and share in His love
For our lives to shine, like the stars above
He wants us to live in a way that's true
To forgive the wrongs that's done to you
To keep pressing onward toward the mark
And to never give up, when the way gets dark
And if we do this, He's faithful and just
To help us through trials and guide us through tests
For it's in the darkness that we need the light
That's when He says walk by faith not by sight
Our vision is narrow and carries less weight
Than His who's Almighty, Majestic, and Great
For as long as we travel this journey through
Let's never forget He cares for you
It helps to remember we're never alone
That God is our Father and Heaven's our home.

THE LIGHTHOUSE

Whatever is in me that shouldn't be
Lord take it away and help me see
The wonderful truths I'd left behind
When I was naive and stagnant in time
May today be the day that I share my beliefs
No drawn out lectures, but simple and brief
Tell a neighbor, a friend, or someone I meet
That Your gift is eternal and Your journey complete
Don't let someone's anger get in the way
To prevent me from saying what You'd have me say
Instead help me reach out in sisterly love
To help someone weaker gain strength from above
Never through boasting and never for greed
May I help someone who's really in need
Give a hug to a child, to a stranger a smile
To an elderly neighbor pay a visit a while
May I never be selfish, but always be kind
When others are hurting help me not to play blind
May the wonderful blessings You've placed upon me
Shine forth in the night to help others see.

THE WEDDING

Your wedding day, a brand new start
A love combined, no missing part
A life of love has reached it's goal
And shone it's light onto your soul
God is smiling down on you
At what is one, no longer two
Those separate lives you use to live
Are now made one to share and give
And as you walked the aisle today
I bowed my head to pause and say
A simple prayer with words of grace
As you took your rightful place
That God would bless the words you'd say
Not just on your wedding day
But days to come and days to go
When the winds of life began to blow
May you refrain from turning back
Though experience you may lack
For every marriage has its moments
Of ups and downs and poor components
But keep the faith, stay strong at heart
Don't let the bad times make you part
Give God a chance to work for you
And He'll keep your wedding vows brand new.

A Mother's Special Prayer

Create in me a clean heart, so that my children see
Streams of living waters flowing out of me
A helping hand, a caring heart, a mother and a friend
When they see me, may they see You and not a life of sin
Help me hug with open arms, my little ones so dear
May what I do and say, reflect Your presence here
Let not their hearts be troubled, nor let them be afraid
Help them see the beauty in all that You have made
For if I fail to teach them the way You'd have them go
Their lives would be empty and Your joy they wouldn't know
So when given special honor when Mother's Day is here
May my children know how precious they are to me all year
And as they give their gifts to show how much they care
May their lives be richly blessed by their mother's special prayer.

I Must Pray

Some say prayers don't matter
I know that's not true
For everything that matters
Begins and ends with You
My life was once in shambles
You came and met my need
It was through prayer
I found You there
You came to me Godspeed
My life required direction
In order to move on
You came to me through prayer
And now my fear is gone
When others were against me
And I'd done nothing wrong
Through prayer You came and rescued me
And helped me be strong
You know all my thoughts
As I go through the day
And I know I was bought with a price I couldn't pay
It helps keep me humble
It helps me obey
In order to stay close to You
I know that I must pray.

Jesus is the Answer

When you're looking for the answer
And trying to find peace
Look my friend to Jesus
His blessings never cease
His power is unlimited
His work is divine
His grace is sufficient
And present all the time
Never give up keep holding His hand
And let Him lead you in following His plan
Sometimes through fire
Sometimes through rain
But He'll never leave you
Alone in your pain
And when God brings you out
Tell others your story
Giving credit to God
And all of His glory.

TOUCHING LIVES

It's not too late for your light to shine
No mountain too high for you to climb
No valley too low that you can't see
Beyond it's dark vicinity
No river so wide that you can't cross
And not one soul that must stay lost
No goal set forth that you can't reach
And there's always someone you can teach
So live your life and live it well
Leave behind a loving trail
And when you do you'll gain so much
Empowered by the lives you've touched.

HERE FOR A MOMENT

Here for a moment
A very brief stay
Then in an instant
He was taken away
My little angel
Was here for a while
Giving us joy
And making us smile
I'm hurting so much
The pain is so deep
I'm choked up inside
I don't want to eat
I'm really exhausted
But still I can't sleep
Father I know he's in Your keeping
But even so I can't stop weeping
I miss his smile
I miss his touch
All those things
I loved so much
Those tiny hands
And tiny feet
That baby scent
And chubby cheeks
Yes Lord this puzzles me
A lot to be exact
I wonder why You blessed me
Then took my blessing back?

To every thing there is a season, and a time to every purpose under the heaven:
Ecclesiastes 3:1 KJV

Keep Me Lord

You're stronger than my enemies
And greater than my sins
You know where I'm going
And you know where I've been
When darkness surrounds me
You're my Guiding Light
You're with me in the morning
And with me in the night
Keep me on the narrow path
Help me not to stray
Let us walk together Lord
As You lead the way
Because of You I'm worthy
You've given me Your best
It's Your grace and mercy
That let's me know I'm blessed.

ONLY YOU CAN

Lord, if You don't feed me, I won't be fed
If you don't lead me, I won't be led
If you don't help me, I won't be helped
And if You don't keep me, I won't be kept.

You Can't Go Wrong With Jesus

~

You can't go wrong with Jesus, no matter what you do
His mercy and grace will always see you through
His guiding hands will lead and show you where to go
He'll take you through trials, and help your faith to grow
You can't go wrong with Jesus, so make up in your mind
To make yourself available and spend with Him some time.

LEARN SOMETHING

This hurt that you're feeling will soon go away
It's here for the moment, but not here to stay
It's come for a season to put you in check
So the wrong you've committed you won't soon forget
Remember our Father is faithful and just
Because He loves us He gives us His best
Nothing we suffer is ever in vain
It comes with a purpose so learn from the pain.

GOD'S LOVE

There's nothing I can do to make You love me more,
Nor to make You love me less
Your love never changes it's always the same,
And Your same is always Your best.

Jesus Christ, the same yesterday, and today, and forever. Hebrews 13:8 KJV

LIVE FOR JESUS

Don't be consumed by the things of this world
Soon they'll pass away
The only thing that will matter then is how you lived today
Did you love everybody?
Did you lend a helping hand?
Did you help one who was hurting?
Did you touch the heart of man?
Did you lift the name of Jesus for all the world to know?
That besides Him there's no other
He's the only way to go
There's a lot to think about
Time is drawing near
For us to die is gain, so death we needn't fear
As Christians on this journey we must live out God's plan
Standing boldly for Him while holding to His hand.

Start with Jesus

∿

Before you start your daily chores make time for the Lord
You're attention He desires your time He adores
Reach beyond your selfishness
Gaze upon His glory
Walk the path of righteousness
Live to tell the story.

OUR FATHER'S HANDS

Don't worry about tomorrow let it be
It's in our Father's hands and so are we
Whatever He has planned is worth the wait
He's always right on time and never late
Remember how He helped you in the past
Your troubles and trials didn't last
He brought you through and proved how much He cared
When you were feeling doubtful, weak, and scared
Consider what He's done for you today
He woke you up led you on your way
Gave you the strength to carry on
Yesterday was here but now it's gone
Hold on to our Father's hand
Even when it's hard to understand
The trials that sometimes come your way
Making it difficult to pray
Know that our Father's on the throne
And though you're going through you're not alone
Christ intercedes and you are heard
Even when you're at a loss for words.

*My Father, who has given them to me, is greater than all, and no one is able
to snatch them out of the Father's hand. John 10:29 ESV*

Multiple Sclerosis

I Move Solely by the strength of God
I Must Survive
I Must Succeed
For God's grace
Outweighs My Struggle

This small and temporary trouble we suffer will bring us a tremendous and eternal glory,
much greater than the trouble. II Corinthians 4:17 Good News Translation

I CAN MAKE IT

I know I can make it with God by my side
No matter how long or bumpy the ride
The Holy Spirit will lead and direct
And will bring to remembrance the things I forget
Like Bible verses to encourage my heart
And the path to take when the way is dark
I choose to follow and not to complain
Nor become bitter because of my pain
Since God allowed this to occur in my life
I trust it's in His plan
So I will not fret, nor will I forget
That my life is in His hands.

Trust in the Lord with all thine heart; and lean not unto thine own understanding. In all thy ways acknowledge Him, and He shall direct thy path. Proverbs 3:5-6 KJV

My Child

It's hard to let you go my child
It's hard to watch you leave
It's hard to watch you walk away
And to another cleave
Although I know it's best for you
And sure to help you grow
I'm shedding tears of missing you
because I love you so
Take with you these words of mine
Hold them in your heart
Stay real close to Jesus
For He will never part
And even though you've moved away
On other grounds to trod
I know you're safe with Jesus
Our Savior and our God.

ONE

Know Jesus, Know God
Know God, Know Jesus.

Jesus saith unto him, Have I been so long time with you, and yet hast thou not known me, Philip? he who hath seen me, hath seen the Father; and how sayest thou then, Show us the Father? John 14:9 KJV

Chosen and Qualified

There's a call on your life and you needn't doubt
That you have the power to carry it out
The job that's ahead is one of great measure
Given by God to bring Him pleasure
Don't be afraid to carry the load
With God by your side you can be bold
When God chose you He did it with pride
So have no doubt you're qualified.

"For many are called, but few are chosen." Matthew 22:14 NKJ

MY HIGHEST PRAISE

My Highest praise belongs to You
Nothing less will ever do
You've blessed me in so many ways
Lord, You deserve my highest praise.

I will bless the Lord at all times: His praise shall continually be in my mouth. Psalms 34:1 KJV

YOU KNOW EVERYTHING

I don't know what the day will bring
I never really do
But one thing is certain
This day belongs to You
You woke me up this morning
You've given me a mind
And I am going to use it
To let my light shine
Out into the darkness
Where evil hides its face
Where every life matters
Regardless of its race
Where nations set before us
Rage and go to war
I will stand for You Lord
And stand for You the more
I don't know what the day will bring
I never really do
But I know You know everything
So I am trusting You.

RUN TO JESUS

Hurting People to and fro
Seem to find me where I go
Keep me Lord within their reach
And with Your leading help me teach
I'll do my best to lend a hand
In trying to help them understand
That what they need is saving grace
And patience Lord, to run this race
Bless us now and give us power
Be our strength and be our tower
If we fall along the way
Pick us up and help us stay
Close to you is my endeavor
By Your side with you forever.

The name of the Lord is a strong tower; the righteous run to it and are safe. Proverbs 18:10 NKJV

BOLD FAITH

Faith when it's tested becomes great
After we pray we learn to wait
As we wait we learn to trust
And learning patience is a must
God helps us to love and obey
Increasing our faith along the way
Nothing's too great for God to do
When our faith is bold
And our walk is true.

Knowing this, that the trying of your faith, worketh patience.
James 1:3 KJV

My Story

If you want a story
One that's tried and true
You can have my story
Of what the Lord can do
He met me on my journey
A long time ago
I let Him in my heart
From there He helped me grow
And now that I'm His child
There is no turning back
He's changed my life forever
My friend, and that's a fact
He's helped me through the hard times
When I was feeling down
He gave to me His peace
When peace could not be found
Sometimes on my journey
I'd hit a dead end road
And felt I couldn't make it
To let the truth be told
He graced me with His mercy
Endowed me with His love
Brought me through the fire
And helped me rise above
I'm no longer captive
I have been set free
To share with you my story
Of what God's done for me.

TRUST GOD

The enemy comes with all its force
To catch you off guard and throw you off course
But just remember he's already doomed
And is not allowed to be in your room
So call on the Father who's more than prepared
To give light in the darkness when you're desperately scared
To bring forth tomorrow
The brightness of day
His light that will guide you and show you the way
Do not be dismayed or taken by grief
Just trust the Father to bring you relief
And when you pray your fervent prayer
Expect the Lord to meet you there
For He's the Holy One indeed
And will always give you what you need.

SOWING SEEDS

Touching lives throughout the races
Putting smiles on people's faces
Mending hearts in broken places
My poetry in motion
Blessing people as I go
Sometimes fast
Sometimes slow
Strangers I may never know
My poetry in motion
Reaching people for the King
Proud to wear His wedding ring
It's all Him no in between
My poetry in motion
My life is His and not my own
I make it plain in every poem
I thank Him for the seeds being sown
Through my poetry in motion.

God's Discipline

Lord, when You chasten
You always let me know
That it's because You love me
And want my faith to grow
You often strike the hardest
Just when morning nears
Then come to reap the harvest
Nourished by my tears
When up against the darkness
Deep within the night
You become my Candle
You become my Light
Lord, it's amazing
How You love me so
To plant a seed of faith in me
And help that faith to grow.

For whom the Lord loves He chastens. Hebrews 12:6 NKJV

REFLECT THE SON

Thank you Lord for the moon at night
For the sun that shines to give us light
For Your Son who came that we might have life
More abundantly
May our hearts comply with who You are
And all You'll ever be
Lord of Lords,
King of Kings,
The One who sets us free
May peace and joy become widespread
As Your Word becomes our daily bread
May we feast on it while being led
By the Holy Spirit
And when it's all said and done
May our lives reflect Your Son
May Your goodness from above
Help us rest within Your love
Knowing all things are possible
Through You.

Therefore, if any man be in Christ, he is a new creature: old things are passed away; behold, all things are become new. II Corinthians 5:17 KJV

HELP LORD

When life is overwhelming
And peace is hard to find
Help me Lord to rest in You
My Heavenly Divine
When storm clouds surround me
And darkness fills my day
Help me put my trust in You
Teach me Lord to pray
When I don't get the answer
That I was hoping for
Let me not grow weary
Help me trust You more
My life is like a whirlwind
The way it spends around
Sometimes up in orbit
And sometimes on the ground
But no matter what I go through
When help is hard to find
I know that I can trust you
To rescue me in time.

FREE FROM ME

Set me free from me Lord
Nothing else will do
I want nothing more
Than to live my life for You
Help me to surrender
Consume me with your fire
May all that I say and do
Be as You desire
Help me know Your voice
So I can plainly hear
Exactly what You're saying
And receive it without fear
Every step I take
Let it be Your will
And when I mustn't move
Help me to be still
I give all the honor
And glory to Your name
Set me free from me Lord
So I'll never be the same.

FEAR NOT

Yesterday
is the day
That you worried about
the day before
Today
is the tomorrow
That you worried about
Yesterday
And tomorrow
will be the day
That you're worrying about
Today.

As confusing as it sounds, so is life when we fail to give our burdens over to God.

Casting all your care upon Him; for He careth for you. I Peter 5:7 KJV

FORGIVEN

You're not the way you used to be
God's made you who you are
Jesus Christ has set you free
And set you free by far
Your past tried to rob you
Tried to break you to the core
But Jesus has erased your past
And remembers it no more
He now says you're forgiven
And shall forever be
No matter what your past was like
You've been redeemed by Thee.

So if the Son sets you free, you will be free indeed. John 8:36 NIV

ENOUGH IS ENOUGH

Come rescue us Lord
This race war is real
Cops killing our Black men
unarmed without steel
And they're allowed to walk free
For days at a time
Only losing their jobs
While we're losing our minds
Injustice runs rampant for people of color
These men being killed were birthed from a mother
Like anyone else
Their Black lives matter
And they deserve justice
In the now not the latter
Let it be known in the U.S. of A
You can kill a Black man and then walk away
You may lose your job, but you'll still get paid
To roam around freely in the mess that you've made
It's not until people take to the streets
With voices and signs
Then tear gas they meet
It's not until people march and protest
That you finally go out and make an arrest
Come quickly Lord, rescue your own
For justice will be served
That every cop who unjustly kills
Will get what he deserves.

For the wrongdoer will be paid back for the wrong he has done, and there is no partiality. Colossians 3:25 ESV

THE GARDEN

Ripe, picked, and ready to go
Are fruits from the garden my dad helped grow
Through toil and labor with compassion for man
He answered the call and then took a stand
He's sown many seeds and watered them too
He's done everything God's called him to do
He stayed in the race and never retired
But kept up the pace as God required
The harvest is plenty, but workers are few
Many are called, but the chosen are true
He answered the dream God placed in his heart
Then stepped out on faith and did his part
He preached the Word as he was led
And when he did the flock was fed
The garden grew because he cared
And fruits going forth because he shared.

*And I heard the voice of the Lord saying, "Whom shall I send, and who will
go for us? Then I said, here am I! Send me." Isaiah 6:8 ESV*

I Love You Dad

Dad I love you dearly
Time has taught me how
I thank God for you daily
I thank God for you now
Your life is full of substance
Not with worldly gain
But with the love of Jesus
Of Whom you're not ashamed
So I've written you this poem
With words I hope will stay
Forever in your heart
Have a Happy Father's Day!

God's Perfect Love

There's not enough praise
To thank God for the days
Of sunshine brought my way
Nor enough time to empty my mind
Of such blessings when I pray
Of all the things I give in return
As far as the eye can see
Nothing could ever begin to repay
The price He paid for me
It would take years from beginning to end
To fulfill the pain He bore
There is no pain to compare to His
For He suffered so much more
So as I live from day to day
Kneeling quietly to pray
Accepting what He brings my way
I cannot fail to see
That God's love is a perfect love
The kind I want in me.

THROUGH HIS EYES

Through His eyes I can start a new life
Become a best friend, become a good wife
Through His eyes I see no wrong
I can forgive and I can be strong
Through His eyes every joy can be sealed
Every broken heart miraculously healed.
Through His eyes I can deny myself
Hold on to His hand when nothing is left
Let go of the sorrow and forget the cause
I can live in today and not in what was
Through His eyes all sin is forgiven
And now I know that life is worth living
Through His eyes.

LIKE A TREE

Lord give me the love that you know I need
You till my heart, and You plant the seed
When You are finished, water me down
Take care of me as I grow from the ground
Nurse me to health when my life is uprooted
When my heart and mind are sick and polluted
Pick me up when I fall to the ground
When my shoulders are sloping, and friends let me down
It is I, Lord, thirsting for love
Needing a blessing from You up above
For I'm like a tree in need of great care
Please nourish me Lord
This is my prayer.

Your Love's Beyond Measure

If ever I get beside myself
And think more than I should
About myself or someone else
Who's done a bit of good
Remind me that the greatest thing
Ever done before
Was when You died and rose again
Now who could ask for more?
No one could ever do
What You have done for us
The giving of Yourself
Has taught us how to trust
Without Your crucifixion and the empty tomb
It'd be just another story that ended all too soon
Now victory is ours because of what You've done
Our sins have been forgiven
Through You
God's Only Son.

A Hurting World

As I pass through life it's sad to see
People in captivity
Broken with no place to go
The unborn killed for birth control
A child abused, a battered wife
A state preparing to end a life
Drug addiction and suicide
Drive by shootings, a loss of pride
Sin is rampant everywhere
It's with us night and day
It may seem slow but it helps to know
That Christ is on His way.

CHANCES

Today is the day for a new beginning
A chance to start over
A chance to stop sinning
A chance to be wise and make the right choices
To obey God and not other voices
Today is the day to swallow your pride
To let go of the hatred you're feeling inside
A chance to be loyal, a chance to be true
A chance to forgive those who've hurt you
A chance to be happy
A chance to repent
A chance to hold on to the Word that God sent
A chance to improve
A chance to achieve
A chance to give and not just receive
Today is the day to let go of self
To walk in the light, though darkness is felt
For tomorrow's not promised
It's today we must fight
To live for God now, and to do what is right.

THE TRUTH

It was not by happenstance my life was turned around,
But Your Holy Word that got me off the ground
It wasn't Uncle's hands that cared for me that night
But You speaking through him that gave me hope and light
It wasn't all the books I'd read or people who came by
For You were always with me Lord, when I began to cry
It wasn't the telephone that got me through the day
It was Your Holy Spirit as I began to pray
You knew all my needs and what was on my mind
As I waited patiently, You rescued me in time.
When I placed my trust in You, the dark clouds passed by
Now unashamed, I praise Your name and tell the people why.

FRIENDS OF THE CROSS

No longer strangers in shades of gray
We met and became friends today
She shared her problems as we talked
I encouraged her as we walked
The tears ran down while she wept
I then gave her a cross I'd kept
I told the truth behind the cross
Of how Jesus suffered to save the lost
That Jesus our Savior came to earth
As a man in the flesh through a virgin birth
He died then arose from the tomb for our freedom
Now satan has lost all power to beat Him
She looked me straight in the eyes
And said she knew the reason why
Jesus Christ was sent to die
That I'd shared with her the truth
And that the empty tomb is proof
Another year has come and gone
My friend and I talk off and on
I share my problems while we talk
She encourages me as we walk
When tears roll down and I feel lost
She points me to our Savior's cross.

SISTERS IN CHRIST

I wrote this poem thinking of you
My sisters in Christ and what we can do
We can change the world if we'd take time out
To share with others what Christ is about
If we just keep the faith as the earth goes around
We could win any race and peace could be found
In the hearts of us women who are willing to give
Unselfishly to help others live
We could stand strong for the sake of the cross
And capture the hearts of those who are lost
As we walk we could lead them and show them the way
By the things that we do, and the words that we say.

GET BUSY

How can I serve You better Lord?
I'd really like to know
His reply was simple
Go where I tell you to go
How can I spend more time with You
To show how much I care?
His reply was simple
Spend time with me in prayer
How can I know You well enough
To follow where You lead?
His reply was simple
I've left my Word, now read
Of all the answers given me
I knew each one was true
Without a doubt, I figured out
The work I had to do.

A Women's Tea Welcome

Inspirations from above
Sent down from our Father's love
To help inspire and motivate
Our precious lives for Jesus sake
So let's sit back and enjoy the time
Just let these moments still your mind
With ears to listen and eyes to see
I welcome you to our women's tea.

Prayer Time

~

It's now I want to pray Lord
And wrap up in Your Love
To thank You for this day
The earth and sky above
My faith in You is crucial
I do not pray in vain
I know Your love is mutual
It saves and keeps me sane
My life seems to be ruined
I do not understand
I don't know why it's happened
I do not know Your plan
But one thing I am sure of
Is that You cannot lie
Someday You might uncover
And reveal the reasons why
For now I'll just sit quietly
Patiently and still
Allowing You the chance
To work in me Your will
My life will continue
With or without man
For You're my loving Father
And I'm the vessel in Your hands.

THE TRUTH ABOUT EASTER

Jesus is Easter in every way said
He died on the cross and arose from the dead
He came to give life and to set sinners free
So He gave up His own for you and for me
With nails in His feet and nails in His hands
He died in a way only God understands
He bore our sins hoping we'd see the light
As to why it was done without hatred or spite
He was here on a mission for a short while
Teaching, preaching, and making men smile
His Father had sent Him, His Only Son
To change this world, and that's what He's done
The truth about Easter is one we must tell
That Christ is not dead, but alive and well.

HIGH SCHOOL GRADUATION

You're blessed to have family and loved ones who care
Blessed to have friends who include you in prayer
Blessed to have those who still keep in touch
Blessed to know God loves you so much
You're blessed beyond measure more than you know
Your heart holds a treasure wherever you go
Remember the good times you've had through the years
The smiles and the laughter you've shared with your peers
For high school is over the new lies ahead
Things will be different, but you needn't dread
For every tomorrow brings a new day
New adventures and people you'll meet on the way
Because life's a gift that's been given to you
Treasure it's memories
The old and the new.

SLOW DOWN

Don't let this world come down on you
And make you feel so small
Remember God cares for you
Which makes you ten feet tall
He will open doors for you
That others cannot touch
Then He alone will guide you through
He loves you just that much
The road you choose to follow
May take you very far
But the road that's straight and narrow
Will lead you to your star
So as you go through life
Keep a steady pace
Trusting in the Lord
To help you win the race
This world may offer power, fortune, and fame
It may put you on the billboards with lights above your name
The truth is this earthly life was never meant to last
It's only temporary and someday it will pass
It's really very simple, but let me make it clear
Your goal should be eternity and not your stay down here.

Follow Your Dream

Follow your dream in all that you do
No dream is ever too big to come true
It's in your believing and not letting go
It's putting in action the things that you know
You have to stay strong, maybe struggle a bit
Your dream may seem far, but just don't you quit
With determination and a prayerful heart
Follow your dream right from the start
Just stay focused, don't go astray
Don't let the negatives stand in your way
Follow your dream, if you have a dream left
Your dream is your own, so believe in yourself.

THE MASCOT

I wore the mask and wore it well
But who I was they couldn't tell
Unless the mask was torn away
Then they'd know my night from day
I've been blessed and I am gifted
Behind this mask when it is lifted
There's a heart that bears my name
It's had its share of hurt and fame
If one must know I bring great pleasure
Behind this mask is unique treasure
For everyone who'd like to see
Behind the mask is really me.

True Gratitude

Many years of service
And what a joy it's been
To have you as our sister
And to know you as our friend
You have been consistent
Serving in our church
You've been so committed
And faithful in your work
A wonderful person
Work ethic full of grace
For years you have served
Within this vital place
And now that you're retiring
We wish you all the best
So please receive our gratitude
From all the lives you've blessed.

God's Creation

A tiny creation from God's own hand
Each breath taken at His command
A life's been given inside a womb
God's tiny one is now in bloom
With legs he'll walk and someday run
With eyes he'll squint them from the sun
With ears he'll hear the bells above
Ringing down His Father's love
So love your little one so dear
Give birth to him or her, don't fear
For every creation God has a plan
We may not see it now, but maybe someday we can.

WISHES

If I had a wish, my wish would be
For a world of peace and unity
That the lame would walk and the blind would see
And all the wars would cease to be
I'd wish for children everywhere
To have a home with parents who care
That there would be no violence there
And they'd never be alone
I'd wish for love to soon replace
The hatred in the human race
So we could all stand face to face
Secure and unafraid
I'd wish for riches to be shared
With people hungry, cold, and scared
I'd wish all babies lives be spared
And not killed before they're born
I mustn't fail to mention
My greatest wish would be
That all would come to Jesus
So He could set them free.

GOD FORGIVES

It hurt me when you let me go
I never got the chance to grow
My life was taken much too soon
For in your life you had no room
For a tiny human being
But that's okay I understand
That Jesus had a better plan
Here with Him is where I live
I love you mom and God forgives.

"If we confess our sins, He is faithful and just and will forgive us our sins and purify us from all unrighteousness." I John 1:9 NIV

JULIE

Your vision is so bright, although you cannot see
It shines a glorious light on others and on me
Your blinded eyes and smiling face encourages the best
To rise above the cares of life and find in God sweet rest
You tap in on important things
Like mother, friend, and wife
And seem to count your blessings
Throughout your daily life
But if for some odd reason, you fall along the way
Remember that in darkness you don't need sight to pray
Know that prayers are answered for those who are sincere
Who walks the straight and narrow
And clings to God so dear
You are very special, to others and to me
Your vision is so bright, although you cannot see
Life is very precious but something greater still
Is for one who's blind to give God time
And walk within His will.

A Pastor's Wife

When married to a pastor
One must understand
It takes a special woman
To love this special man
An asset to his calling
A gift of pure delight
Someone who walks beside him
And models what is right
When married to a pastor
She too bares the pain
When members turn against him
And scandalize his name
It takes a special woman to stand by his side
At funerals and wakes of those who have died
Some things required for a pastor to do
Would seem much harder if it wasn't for you
So just keep praying and doing your best
To love him through trials and love him through tests
God chose you to share in his life
You're a vessel of honor-
A pastor's wife.

No Perfect Church

The church doors are open wide
Come and have a seat inside
Here where you can worship friend
And on the altar leave your sins
Free to sing and free to pray
Free to worship your own way
All can come, no color line
You just need an open mind
Don't let satan keep you out
Neither let him steal your shout
Receive God's Word, receive it well
It can save your soul from hell
So don't let others steal your joy
By what they say or do
Instead, keep attending church
And let your walk be true
My friend stop running
It's time to end your search
For no matter where you go
You won't find a perfect church.

OUR PASTOR'S WIFE

An attitude of selflessness
An ever smiling face
A woman on a mission
A woman full of grace
A woman who's a leader
Walking in the light
A woman meek and humble
Trying to live right
A woman of wisdom
Sent from above
Witnessing Christ
And sharing His love
What more must I say
You're a jewel in this life
It's an honor to know you
Our Pastor's Wife.

TODAY

Today my friend went home to stay
I'm at a loss for words to say
My heart grew full
My insides cried
When I was told that he had died
I knelt beside my bed in prayer
I always meet my Savior there
I spoke to Him it went like this
Help me Lord, this friend I'll miss
Help his family make them strong
Fill their empty hearts with song
Let them cry, and cry it through
Let them know You love them too
Please Lord hear their bitter sob
The one that cries, why, why, God?
Why take him and not another
Why my son, why my brother?
Then answer in Your gentle voice
Today he was the man of choice
He was before the world began
This was his time, this was My plan
Here with Me he's found sweet rest
Completely free, completely blessed
This my friend, I hope is treasured
This joy he's found cannot be measured
Just talk to Me each day in prayer
I promise you will find Me there

For I will never let you go
Your loved one's joy you'll always know
And day by day, I'll comfort you
I'll hold your hand and see you through.

The Lord is close to the brokenhearted and saves those who are crushed in spirit. Psalms 34:18 NIV

THE SUN WILL SHINE AGAIN

The words I'm sorry, a warm embrace
Will never fill that empty space
But as a friend I'm standing by
To tell you it's alright to cry
Someday the sun will shine again
The clouds will pass, and the rain will end
Although it's hard to face today
This pain you feel will go away
Just enough to let you know
Sometimes our loses help us grow
I know it's hard to see the light
But it's still there, just not as bright
And when you miss the one you love
Rely on comfort from above
Call on the One who died for you
He understands and will see you through.

The Lord is close to the brokenhearted and saves those who are crushed in spirit. Psalms 34:18 NIV

HAZEL

Someday I'll awake in Heaven and see her lovely face
She smiled so very often and gave such warm embrace
She always wore a smile although sometimes in pain
I loved to hear her voice when she would call my name
It seems like it was yesterday I called her on the phone
I told her I loved her, but didn't talk too long
I told her I would pray for her and she believed I would
Because of her belief in me, I prayed the best I could
I left her in my Father's hands, I knew He knew the way
If it was best to take her home with Him, or best to let her stay
It wasn't very long before the answer came
As I brought it to a close in Jesus precious name
She's gone now, I'll miss her, yes I will
But I believe if she could speak
She'd tell us Heaven's real!

LOVE, LAURA

⁓

Just a word before I go
I want my daddy Dave to know
The situation I was in
Has led me to a special Friend
One whose arms are full of grace
Whose love has easily replaced
The pain that I was dealt
My Friend has also felt
Forgiveness is a must
If you ever want to trust
Let go and loose the chain
Which is holding in the pain
Keep me in your heart
And you'll never lose that part of me
Which helped your world go round
Just remember what I've spoken
And accept it as a token
Maybe then you'll find this Friend whom
I have found.

ETERNITY AT BEST

I once was young but now I'm old
Was once for sale, but now I'm sold
Jesus Christ bought all of me
He paid the price on Calvary
He gave up all He could give
He shed His blood so I could live
Now as I look back in time
I realize He was always mine
Along life's road He gives relief
I find in Him great strength and peace
A song that makes the heavens ring
Whenever I begin to sing
Mighty Father near and far
I'm so glad You're who You are
I'm glad You came through Heaven's gate
Into my heart and not too late
You've been with me in stormy winds
My one and only lasting Friend
No one ever took Your place
Now I get to see Your face
I once was young, but now I'm old
This is where true life unfolds
It's in Your bosom I will rest
And live eternity at best.

SOMEDAY

Someday we will leave this place
And leave our cares behind
When we appear before Jesus' face
Oh, what a joyous time!
Heaven then will be our home
Don't you want to go?
To gather around our Savior's throne
And leave this world below
Let's keep this thought within our hearts
As we go throughout each day
Let us live what Jesus taught
In all we do and say
Let's walk this journey reassured
That we are not alone
For Jesus loves us more than life
That's why He gave His own.

HEAVEN

No more sorrow
No more pain
No more guilt
No more shame
No more lack
Only gain
Now you know true joy.

I Offer You Jesus

I offer you Jesus the only help I know
The One who saves and heals
And helps our faith to grow
The One who paid the penalty
For every single sin
The One who cleans our slate
And helps us start again
I offer you Jesus
The One who has the power
To deliver us from evil
In our darkest hour
The One who holds the keys
Of life and death in hand
The One who has the answers
When we don't understand
I offer you Jesus
In all I say and do
I've given Him my life
Would you give Him yours too?

While it is said: "Today, if you will hear His voice, Do not harden your heart as in the rebellion." Hebrews 3:15 NKJV

Printed in the United States
By Bookmasters